10 -17

KNOW YOUR FOOD

FATS AND CHOLESTEROL

KNOW YOUR FOOD

Fats and Cholesterol

Fiber

Flavorings, Colorings, and Preservatives

Food Safety

Genetically Modified Foods

Gluten

Organic Foods

Protein

Salt

Starch and Other Carbohydrates

Sugar and Sweeteners

Vitamins and Minerals

Water

KNOW YOUR FOOD

Fats and Cholesterol

JOHN PERRITANO

MASON CREST

Mason Crest
450 Parkway Drive, Suite D
Broomall, PA 19008
www.masoncrest.com

MTM Publishing, Inc.
435 West 23rd Street, #8C
New York, NY 10011
www.mtmpublishing.com

President: Valerie Tomaselli
Vice President, Book Development: Hilary Poole
Designer: Annemarie Redmond
Copyeditor: Peter Jaskowiak
Editorial Assistant: Leigh Eron

Series ISBN: 978-1-4222-3733-5
Hardback ISBN: 978-1-4222-3734-2
E-Book ISBN: 978-1-4222-8041-6

Library of Congress Cataloging-in-Publication Data
Names: Perritano, John, author.
Title: Fats and cholesterol / by John Perritano.
Description: Broomall, PA: Mason Crest, [2018] | Series: Know your food |
    Audience: Ages 12+ | Audience: Grades 7 to 8. | Includes bibliographical
    references and index.
Identifiers: LCCN 2017000430 (print) | LCCN 2017001754 (ebook) | ISBN
    9781422237342 (hardback: alk. paper) | ISBN 9781422280416 (ebook)
Subjects: LCSH: Fatty acids in human nutrition—Juvenile literature. |
    Cholesterol—Juvenile literature.
Classification: LCC QP752.F3 P47 2018 (print) | LCC QP752.F3 (ebook) | DDC
    613.2/84—dc23
LC record available at https://lccn.loc.gov/2017000430

Printed and bound in the United States of America.

First printing
9 8 7 6 5 4 3 2 1

TABLE OF CONTENTS

Series Introduction 6

Chapter One: What Are Fats and Cholesterol? 9

Chapter Two: History, Manufacture, and Use 23

Chapter Three: Medical Concerns 31

Chapter Four: Consuming Fats 45

Further Reading 55

Series Glossary 57

Index 59

About the Author 64

Photo Credits 64

Key Icons to Look for:

Words to Understand: These words with their easy-to-understand definitions will increase the reader's understanding of the text, while building vocabulary skills.

Sidebars: This boxed material within the main text allows readers to build knowledge, gain insights, explore possibilities, and broaden their perspectives by weaving together additional information to provide realistic and holistic perspectives.

Educational Videos: Readers can view videos by scanning our QR codes, which will provide them with additional educational content to supplement the text. Examples include news coverage, moments in history, speeches, iconic sports moments, and much more.

Text-Dependent Questions: These questions send the reader back to the text for more careful attention to the evidence presented there.

Research Projects: Readers are pointed toward areas of further inquiry connected to each chapter. Suggestions are provided for projects that encourage deeper research and analysis.

Series Glossary of Key Terms: This back-of-the-book glossary contains terminology used throughout the series. Words found here increase the reader's ability to read and comprehend higher-level books and articles in this field.

SERIES INTRODUCTION

In the early 19th century, a book was published in France called *Physiologie du goût* (*The Physiology of Taste*), and since that time, it has never gone out of print. Its author was Jean Anthelme Brillat-Savarin. Brillat-Savarin is still considered to be one of the great food writers, and he was, to use our current lingo, arguably the first "foodie." Among other pearls, *Physiologie du goût* gave us one of the quintessential aphorisms about dining: "Tell me what you eat, and I will tell you what you are."

This concept was introduced to Americans in the 20th century by a nutritionist named Victor Lindlahr, who wrote simply, "You are what you eat." Lindlahr interpreted the saying literally: if you eat healthy food, he argued, you will become a healthy person.

But Brillat-Savarin likely had something a bit more metaphorical in mind. His work suggested that the dishes we create and consume have not only nutritional implications, but ethical, philosophical, and even political implications, too.

To be clear, Brillat-Savarin had a great deal to say on the importance of nutrition. In his writings he advised people to limit their intake of "floury and starchy substances," and for that reason he is sometimes considered to be the inventor of the low-carb diet. But Brillat-Savarin also took the idea of dining extremely seriously. He was devoted to the notion of pleasure in eating and was a fierce advocate of the importance of being a good host. In fact, he went so far as to say that anyone who doesn't make an effort to feed his guests "does not deserve to have friends." Brillat-Savarin also understood that food was at once deeply personal and extremely social. "Cooking is one of the oldest arts," he wrote, "and one that has rendered us the most important service in civic life."

Modern diners and cooks still grapple with the many implications of Brillat-Savarin's most famous statement. Certainly on a nutritional level, we understand that a diet that's low in fat and high in whole grains is a key to healthy living. This is no minor issue. Unless our current course is reversed, today's "obesity epidemic" is poised to significantly reduce the life spans of future generations.

Meanwhile, we are becoming increasingly aware of how the decisions we make at supermarkets can ripple outward, impacting our neighborhoods, nations, and the earth as a whole. Increasing numbers of us are demanding organically produced foods and ethically sourced ingredients. Some shoppers reject products that contain artificial ingredients like trans fats or high-fructose corn syrup. Some adopt gluten-free or vegan diets, while others "go Paleo" in the hopes of returning to a more "natural" way of eating. A simple trip to the supermarket can begin to feel like a personality test—the implicit question is not only "what does a *healthy* person eat?," but also "what does a *good* person eat?"

The Know Your Food series introduces students to these complex issues by looking at the various components that make up our meals: carbohydrates, fats, proteins, vitamins, and so on. Each volume focuses on one component and explains its function in our bodies, how it gets into food, how it changes when cooked, and what happens when we consume too much or too little. The volumes also look at food production—for example, how did the food dye called Red No. 2 end up in our food, and why was it taken out? What are genetically modified organisms, and are they safe or not? Along the way, the volumes also explore different diets, such as low-carb, low-fat, vegetarian, and gluten-free, going beyond the hype to examine their potential benefits and possible downsides.

Each chapter features definitions of key terms for that specific section, while a Series Glossary at the back provides an overview of words that are most important to the set overall. Chapters have Text-Dependent Questions at the end, to help students assess their comprehension of the most important material, as well as suggested Research Projects that will help them continue their exploration. Last but not least, QR codes accompany each chapter; students with cell phones or tablets can scan these codes for videos that will help bring the topics to life. (Those without devices can access the videos via an Internet browser; the addresses are included at the end of the Further Reading list.)

In the spirit of Brillat-Savarin, the volumes in this set look beyond nutrition to also consider various historical, political, and ethical aspects of food. Whether it's the key role that sugar played in the slave trade, the implications of industrial meat production in the fight against climate change, or the short-sighted political decisions that resulted in the water catastrophe in Flint, Michigan, the Know Your Food series introduces students to the ways in which a meal can be, in a real sense, much more than just a meal.

WHAT ARE FATS AND CHOLESTEROL?

WORDS TO UNDERSTAND

arteries: blood vessels that transport blood from the heart to all parts of the body.

calories: units of energy.

carbohydrates: starches, sugars, and fibers found in food; a main source of energy for the body.

diabetes: a disease in which the body's ability to produce the hormone insulin is impaired.

macronutrients: any substance required in large amounts by living organisms.

metabolize: the way the body processes food into energy.

obesity: a condition in which excess body fat has amassed to the point where it causes ill-health effects.

protein: a nutrient found in meats and other foods that are essential to all living organisms.

Have you ever eaten a quarter-stick of butter? Doesn't sound very appetizing, does it? Consider this: if you're an average American teenage male, then the amount of fat you consume every day is equal to that quarter-pound of butter. Teenage girls rejoice—on average, you eat much less.

Baked goods wouldn't be the same without fat.

Many foods we love, including cupcakes, peanuts, cheese, milk, beef, pork, sour cream, vegetable oil, cookies, cakes, and dark chicken meat have a high fat content. All these foods are tasty, yet for most people, *f-a-t* may as well be a four-letter word. It's synonymous with bad health, bulging waistlines, tight jeans, and clogged arteries.

The reason is simple: eating too much fat can make a person sick. It can even kill. Excess fat can cause a person to be overweight, or suffer from **obesity**, **diabetes**, heart disease, high blood pressure, and a variety of other ailments. In fact, too much fat in our diet is so bad that doctors tell us to stay away from it.

Yet we can't live without fat. That's because fat is one of the three macronutrients that sustain life. Fats, along with carbohydrates and proteins, provide our bodies with the fuel our cells need to function. That's because fat is a rich source of calories, and our bodies turn those calories into energy. Without that energy, our organs and muscles wouldn't function as they should.

Fats transports certain vitamins, such as Vitamins A, D, E, and K, through the bloodstream, sending them straight to our muscles and organs. These and other vitamins and nutrients are critical for good health. They are not soluble in water but are easily dissolved in fat.

Fat, believe it or not, also keeps us from eating too much. Since our bodies digest fat more slowly than other nutrients, our stomachs and intestines remain "fuller" after a meal. They don't send out hunger signals to the brain, which is the reason we feel satisfied after chowing down on a meal rich in fat.

The fat in ice cream gives it a rich texture.

EDUCATIONAL VIDEO

FAT BASICS

Scan this code for a video about fat.

Moreover, fat tastes good. It makes food smoother, juicier, and more tender. Butter is rich in fat and has a creamy taste. We smother it on vegetables and bread. We put it on mashed potatoes. Fat makes puddings creamier and baked goods more tasty.

Fat is in your refrigerator, and not just in the butter dish. It's in the frozen pizza and ice cream. It's in your cupboard, in cans of soup, bags of chips, and packages of cookies. Of the 100 to 150 grams of fat Americans eat on average each day, more than 60 percent is hidden in foods.

CHEWING THE FAT

When people hear the word "fat," they automatically think of types of fat they can see, such as the white jelly-like stuff around the edges of a steak, or the rolls of jiggly flesh around a person's belly, thighs, and arms. It's true, those are forms of fat, but there's much more to fat than what's visible.

Fat is the way humans and animals store energy. Fat comes from the food we eat, and we store some fat to keep us going when supplies run low. Our bodies burn fat when we need energy. It provides us with essential fatty acids that the body cannot manufacture itself.

Fat also serves as a warehouse for extra calories. When the body uses up all its calories from carbohydrates, the body reaches into its warehouse to burn calories from fat. Fat makes skin healthy and hair luxurious. It insulates us from the cold and protects our organs from damage.

The lines of fat in steak are called marbling; marbling makes steak juicier and more flavorful.

TYPES OF CHOLESTEROL

Fat goes hand-in-hand with another substance, called cholesterol. Cholesterol is fatty and wax-like. It produces hormones and other substances that help a person digest food. However, the body makes all the cholesterol it needs—in fact, many people actually make more than they need. Cholesterol levels increase even further if a person eats a high-fat diet.

Not all types of cholesterol are the same—some is considered good, and some bad. The "good cholesterol" is *high-density lipoprotein* (HDL). HDL removes bad cholesterol from blood vessels and carries it back to the liver, where the body can then expel it.

LDL, or *low-density lipoprotein*, is known as "bad cholesterol" because it can clog a person's arteries and restrict blood flow to the heart. LDL cholesterol also produces plaque, which can keep blood from flowing through the body, creating a barrier that

GLYCERIDES AND LIPIDS

Most of the fat found in nature belongs to a group called *glycerides*. The fat on a ham or steak is an example of a glyceride. Glycerides are known as simple lipids, which is another term for fat. They're "simple" because they contain only carbon, hydrogen, and oxygen atoms. Lipids can store twice as much energy as proteins and carbohydrates. When lipids combine with oxygen from the air, they release energy, which allows us to move our muscles or digest our food.

Compound lipids are fatty substances that hold on to something else, such as cholesterol. For example, triglycerides are a type of fat that is transported in the blood. It is the most abundant fatty molecule in your body. Whatever calories your body doesn't burn right away are turned into triglycerides, which are then stored in fat cells. Triglycerides also contain cholesterol. More than 90 percent of the fats in food are triglycerides. An elevated level of triglycerides may lead to heart disease.

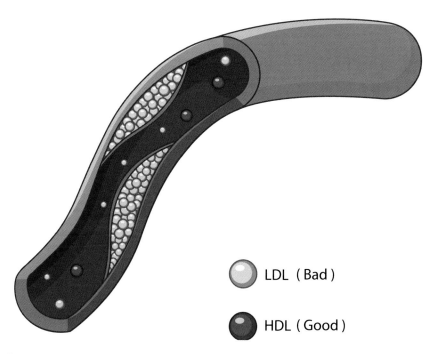

LDL (Bad)

HDL (Good)

This illustration shows the difference between HDL, which moves through the bloodstream, and LDL, which can clog the arteries.

blood cannot pass through. Too much plaque can make the heart work a lot harder than it has to as it pumps blood through the body.

A bit of plaque can also break off and form a blood clot. A person can get a stroke if one of those clots walls off any artery moving blood to the brain. A stroke can result in partial paralysis, slurred speech, and death. A person can have a heart attack if a clot blocks an artery to the heart.

SATURATED AND UNSATURATED FATS

Fat is composed of chains of chemical compounds made of fatty acids. Each fatty acid contains atoms of carbon, hydrogen, and oxygen. Some fatty acids have only a few carbon atoms, while others can have more than 20. The most common fatty acid

Olive oil is a healthy monounsaturated fat.

contains 18 carbon atoms. Fatty acids are important sources of energy and help us metabolize our food, or turn it into energy.

Fatty acids come in three different varieties: *saturated*, *monounsaturated*, and *polyunsaturated*. Although each is composed of the same type of atoms, their makeup is slightly different.

Sometimes the hydrogen, carbon, and oxygen atoms in fat arrange themselves into solids. That type of fat is called *saturated*. It used to be that scientists considered saturated fat to be a "bad fat," medically speaking. That's because they believed that saturated fat raises cholesterol levels. However, current research indicates that saturated fat may also raise the levels of HDL cholesterol in the bloodstream, while lowering the level of triglycerides, a type of fat that is transported in the blood. Both can counter the effects of heart disease.

Because saturated fats are dense, they stay solid at room temperature. Foods such as red meat, cheese, and butter contain saturated fats. Any excess saturated fat can be harmful, because our bodies make all the saturated fat we need.

Unsaturated fat is often called "good fat," because it is essential to a healthy heart. Fish oil, nuts, and olive oil are examples of foods that contain unsaturated fat.

Monounsaturated and polyunsaturated fats are two types of unsaturated fat. Research shows that both can improve a person's blood cholesterol levels, decreasing the risk of heart disease. We normally consume polyunsaturated fats from plant oils, such canola oil. One type of polyunsaturated fat that is beneficial to heart health is omega-3. Fish are good sources of omega-3, as are nuts.

REALLY, REALLY BAD FAT

French fries! Love 'em! How about cupcakes and donuts, puddings and chocolate cake. Can't live without them. All are so tasty, as are fried chicken wings and fried jalapeño poppers. Can food that taste so good be bad for you? The answer is an unequivocal "yes." That's because all those foods, plus many more, often contain *trans fats*.

Trans fats are the worst type of unsaturated fat a person can consume. Some trans fats occur naturally in the stomach and intestines of animals. For example, milk and meat products contain minimal traces of trans fats. However, much of the trans fat that people consume is artificial. That means they're made in a laboratory by humans.

The food processing industry creates trans fats through a process called *hydrogenation*, a procedure in which hydrogen is added to liquid vegetable oils to make them more firm. Cookies, cakes, baked goods, and other products made with hydrogenated vegetable oil can sit on a grocery store shelf or in your cupboard for a long time without spoiling. Hydrogenation also creates a desirable texture. Many fast-food restaurants use trans fats to deep-fry foods, like chicken wings and french fries, because the oils can be reused.

Trans fats are bad because they can raise a person's bad cholesterol levels and lower good cholesterol levels, which can lead to an increased risk of heart disease and diabetes. Most fried food and most processed food is laden with trans fats.

Dariush Mozaffarian, a cardiologist at Harvard University, knows the danger of consuming trans fats. In 2006, Mozaffarian and other researchers looked at the impact that trans fats had on human health. They concluded that if Americans cut most of the artificial trans fats from their diets, between 72,000 and 228,000 fewer people would die from heart attacks and heart disease each year. For every 2 percent increase in calories from trans fats, the researchers reported, there was a corresponding 23 percent higher risk of coronary heart disease.

French fries are delicious but unhealthy because of all the fat they contain.

SATURATED FAT CONSUMPTION

 Adult men, on average, eat 81 grams of fat per day, while teenage males consume 91 grams. Adult women consume 64 grams; girls and teenage females, 51 grams. According to the American Heart Association, a person should limit the amount of saturated fats to less than 7 percent of their total daily caloric intake. A person that consumes 2,000 calories a day, for example, should only consume about 16 grams of saturated fat.

"Artificial trans fats are a dangerous additive in our food supply. Artificial trans fats have no nutritional value, have great potential for harm, and can be easily replaced by natural fats and oils without compromising food taste, price, or availability," Mozaffarian told the New York City Board of Health at the time of the study.

BAN THE FAT

Trans fat is so bad for you that people want to ban it, to get it out of our diets entirely. At first, partially hydrogenated oils were believed safer than the animal fats they replaced. But by the 1970s and the 1980s, scientific studies seemed to suggest that trans fats were unhealthy. Still, the Food and Drug Administration (FDA), the U.S. government agency that regulates food and drugs, decided at the time that just the opposite was true.

By the early 1990s and well into the 2000s, however, scientists proved time and again that trans fats and saturated fats were responsible for heart disease and other problems. For example:

- *The American Journal of Clinical Nutrition* in 2013 linked trans-fat consumption to increased mortality rates.

Labels on food packaging inform consumers about how much fat is in a product and, importantly, which types of fat.

- A 2014 study showed that adults who ate food fried in trans-fat oil four to six times a week were 23 percent more likely to develop coronary artery disease

- Partially hydrogenated soybean oils raised cholesterol levels by 15 percent compared to regular soybean and canola oils in people whose bad cholesterol levels were elevated.

In 2006, the FDA got onboard with the mountain of scientific evidence. At the time it required food manufacturers to list the amount of trans fats on food labels. By 2015 the FDA had gone even further, ordering the removal of trans fats from the food supply by 2018.

In 2014 the World Health Organization (WHO), an arm of the United Nations, called for a complete ban on trans fats throughout Europe. According to the WHO, 50 percent of European adults are overweight and obese, although in many countries, that figure is closer to 70 percent.

The WHO says that 57.4 percent of adults who are 20 years old or older are overweight or obese. Moreover, an estimated 320,000 men and women in 20 Western European countries die every year because they are obese or overweight.

The goal of the WHO is to "develop and implement national policies to ban or virtually eliminate trans fats from the food supply, with a view to making the European Region trans-fat free. Although progress has been made in reducing this component, popular foods with high amounts of trans fats are still readily available."

TEXT-DEPENDENT QUESTIONS

1. What are trans fats?
2. Which type of fat is a "good fat?"
3. What are the harmful health effects of high cholesterol?

RESEARCH PROJECT

Keep track of the amount of fat and cholesterol you consume in packages of food, candy, and baked goods you eat for seven days. You can do this by reading nutritional labels on each item. Each nutritional label will list these items: Calories from Fat, Total Fat, Saturated Fat, Trans Fat, and Cholesterol. When the week has concluded, use the information you gathered and put it into a bar chart. What did you learn? What can you conclude?

CHAPTER

2

HISTORY, MANUFACTURE, AND USE

 ### WORDS TO UNDERSTAND

caul: the fatty tissue covering the intestines of a cow, sheep, or pig.

Industrial Age: the period from about the late 1700s through the 1800s, when the manufacturing process moved from the home to mechanized factories.

kindred: alike.

primates: mammals, including humans and apes, who have hand-like feet, hands, and forward-facing eyes.

W e often take grocery shopping for granted. Whether it's a frozen pizza, a can of stew, or a dozen eggs, any food we might want is on the store shelf for purchase. It wasn't always like that, of course.

Our early ancestors couldn't go to the grocery store. They were hunters and gatherers who ate pretty much what they found. In northern climates, that meant consuming a diet rich in animal fat, while those living near the equator chowed down mostly on plants, which were available year round.

Still, humans craved meat. Specifically, they craved the protein and fat that meat provided. Why is that? Unlike other animals, humans have large, complicated brains

Emperor Napoleon III knew the importance of a tasty fat source.

that require a lot of energy to run properly. Humans needed to feed their brains, so to speak. They ate more and more and more fat-rich meat. Meat contained protein, vitamins, and fatty acids that their brains needed to grow.

Because our early ancestors couldn't stop at the local drive-through to get a bacon double cheeseburger, they had to find this meat by finding and killing animals. That meant they needed fat to provide the energy for hunting. Soon, humans became the fattest of all **primates**. That same evolutionary process continues today.

In fact, we modern humans prefer lipid-rich foods, not because of any evolutionary requirement, but because they smell and taste good. In fact, people love fatty foods so much that if there's a shortage of a certain type of fat, let's say butter, people start to panic.

That's what happened in the 1800s in France. At the time, France was in the throes of a butter shortage caused by the **Industrial Age**. As farmers moved from the countryside into the cities to find work in factories, butter supplies dwindled and prices soared, leading to a butter shortage. Some products, especially meat and butter, were too expensive for most working-class people.

In 1869, Emperor Napoleon III of France needed a replacement for butter, and he needed it fast. So he held a contest. He asked his subjects to come up with an inexpensive substitute for butter. The idea for the contest, according to a 1925 story in the *Boston Medical and Surgical Journal*, was to "furnish sailors and people of limited means with a cheap, wholesome fat of high dietetic value."

As soon as the contest was announced, a French chemist named Hippolyte Mège-Mouriès went to work. Born in 1817, Mège-Mouriès started his career in science when he was 16. Years later, he began studying food, and he soon developed a calcium phosphate product from cows that he marketed as a health food.

In 1869 Mège-Mouriès created a butter substitute from beef fat, water, and milk fat. He called the whitish-looking substance *oleomargarine*. *Oleum* is the Latin name for beef fat, and *margarite* is Greek for pearl. Thus, margarine was born. It was smooth like butter. It was as tasty as butter, but less expensive. And in France, a crisis had been averted.

THE BUTTER WARS

Other scientists soon began tinkering with margarine's formula. Over time, they replaced the beef fat with vegetable oils, such as cottonseed and soybean. Margarine arrived in the United States in the 1870s, much to the horror of dairy farmers.

Within 10 years, more than 30 margarine companies had opened, setting off a civil war between them and dairy farmers. The farmers were understandably upset: scientists had upended the market by creating a butter alternative that was inexpensive. The butter industry was about to go bust, forcing the dairy industry to spend a lot of money to convince lawmakers to ban the sale of margarine.

Politicians from states dependent on dairy led the battle against butter's new competition. Minnesota's governor, Lucius Hubbard, railed that "the ingenuity of depraved human genius has culminated in the production of oleomargarine and

EDUCATIONAL VIDEO

BUTTER VERSUS MARGARINE

Scan this code for a video about the differences between the two.

A 1948 advertisement from the magazine Ladies Home Journal *shows how to add color to margarine.*

its kindred abominations." In nearby Wisconsin, Senator Joseph Quarles said, "I want butter that has the natural aroma of life and health. I decline to accept as a substitute caul fat, matured under the chill of death, blended with vegetable oils and flavored by chemical tricks."

Flexing its political muscle, the dairy industry convinced lawmakers in New York, Michigan, Maine, Pennsylvania, Ohio, and Wisconsin to ban the sale of yellow-colored margarine. The margarine makers sued, and a court overruled the ban in New York.

The butter wars then shifted to Congress. In 1886, Congress passed the Margarine Act, which instituted steep fees and taxes on margarine manufacturers.

By 1902, 32 states had imposed color restrictions on margarine. Some, like Vermont and New Hampshire, required margarine to be colored pink so people would know that it was not butter. Other states proposed dying yellow margarine brown, red, and even black. The U.S. Supreme Court eventually overturned these "pink laws," although the ban on yellow margarine remained. Wisconsin—not coincidentally, the Dairy State— was the last state to repeal its ban on yellow margarine—it scrapped the law in 1967.

THE BIRTH OF HYDROGENATION

One of the downsides of natural fats is that they can spoil fairly quickly. In 1902 a German scientist named Wilhelm Normann discovered that if he added hydrogen to cottonseed oil under intense heat and pressure, he could make a new type of solid fat that was less likely to spoil than other fats. Little did Normann know that the process, hydrogenation, would revolutionize the food industry, but also create health problems for generations of consumers.

The product Normann invented looked like creamy animal lard. He brought his concoction to a soap and candle company named Proctor & Gamble, which began selling the product under the brand name Crisco. The name was derived from "crystallized cottonseed oil."

The name Crisco comes from "crystallized cottonseed oil."

THE STATE OF FAT

Some foods, like peanuts and butter, are loaded with fat. Others, like carrots and apples, are not. But what are the fattiest foods in the United States? The website health.com put together a list of the various food concoctions in each state that are incredibly high in fat. Here are five of them:

- **Arkansas**: A catfish, smothered in cornmeal, flour, and eggs, packs a gut-busting 24 grams of fat per serving. That doesn't include the side dishes of deep-fried hush puppies.
- **Illinois**: Deep-dish pizza. One serving of the cheese and tomato pie has more than 40 grams of fat, 5 more than the recommended daily limit.
- **Massachusetts**: Chocolate chip cookies. There's one bakery in the Bay State that sells a cookie containing 19 grams of fat, and 10 of those grams are saturated fat.
- **New Jersey**: What do you get when combine fried chicken fingers, mozzarella sticks, french fries, a roll, and marinara sauce together? You get a sandwich with an estimated 45 grams of fat.
- **New York**: The Quadruple Bypass Burger. Made of home fries, macaroni salad, french fries, and other ingredients, including either hamburger meat, hot dogs, or sausage, this burger has an estimated 93 grams to 203 grams of fat.

Crisco didn't spoil, and millions of cooks began using it for baking, frying, and cooking food. Touted as an "economical alternative to animal fats and butter," Crisco was an immediate success. It was also the first manufactured food to contain trans fat.

TRANS FATS ON THE MARCH

Crisco, along with another new type of fat called partially hydrogenated vegetable oil, became very popular in the United States during World War II. At the time, butter was in short supply and was even rationed. Americans used margarine made from hydrogenated vegetable oil to cook with.

When the war ended, the fast-food craze began. During that period, the United States found itself the wealthiest nation on the planet. People now had money to buy things—including automobiles—that were out of their financial reach during the war and the Great Depression.

People became more mobile and, as a result, fast-food restaurants, such as McDonald's, began springing up all over the country to feed hungry travelers. Partially hydrogenated oil was perfect for fast-food cooking, especially frying foods. It was cheap. It had a long shelf life. It could be used over and over again. It also made french fries and other fried treats tastier.

TEXT-DEPENDENT QUESTIONS

1. Who invented margarine?
2. What are some of the benefits of trans fats for food manufacturers?
3. Explain the process of hydrogenation.

RESEARCH PROJECT

Go through a food magazine and cut out 10 to 15 pictures of the different types of food you see, such as pies, ice cream, vegetables, fruits, pancakes, and so on. Based on what you have read about saturated and unsaturated fats so far, categorize each based on their type of fat.

CHAPTER 3

MEDICAL CONCERNS

 ## WORDS TO UNDERSTAND

adipose: a type of body tissue used for the storage of fat.

atherosclerosis: hardening of the arteries, which slowly blocks blood flow.

hormones: substances produced by the body that instruct cells and tissues to perform certain functions.

Every time we eat a juicy steak, ham, or pork chop, we store the fat contained in those foods so our bodies can use it later as energy. As you read earlier, fat does a number of things. It insulates us against the cold and it protects our vital organs. It also helps us to grow, reproduce, and fight off infection.

Our bodies do quite a juggling act when it comes to making, metabolizing, storing, and using fat. If something is thrown out of whack, the effects can be devastating. A person can suffer from heart disease, diabetes, and a wide range of other ailments. For instance, too many triglycerides in your blood system can put you at risk for clogged arteries, which can lead to a deadly stroke or a heart attack.

Why can fat be dangerous?

Fat can be stored in any cell in our body, although most fat is packed into special cells called *adipose cells*, or fat cells. Fat cells look like ordinary cells. However, once these cells become infused with fat, they expand. They get larger and, yes, fatter.

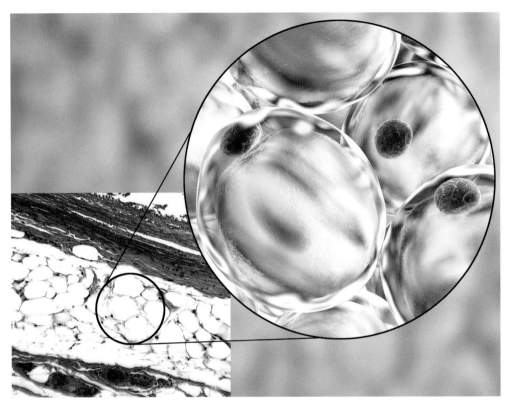

Adipose tissue.

Fat cells group together to form fatty tissue known as **adipose** tissue. Adipose tissue is thick and yellowish. It is the grizzle that we slice off a cooked steak and the "love handles" around our hips. Not every person has the same amount of fat, however. Women typically have more fat than men. A quarter of a woman's body is made of fat, while the average man's body is 12 to 16 percent fat.

Moreover, adipose tissue is not spread out evenly. Men tend to store more fat tissue around their abdomens, while women store fat around their thighs, buttocks, and hips. A man with plenty of stored fat around his abdomen is said to have a "beer belly." The shape of his body is often compared to an apple. A woman with excess fat generally has a body shaped like a pear. Muscles can also store fat, which the body can then use for quick energy.

TOO MUCH FAT

Fat becomes a big problem when there's simply too much of it in our bodies, especially saturated fats. Let's review: fats are made from carbon, hydrogen, and oxygen atoms. Saturated fats have a lot of hydrogen atoms, which makes the chain of fatty acids dense and rigid. Trans fats—artificially made fat—adds additional hydrogen atoms to saturated fat, so it is extremely dense. Saturated fat can lead to obesity, one of the biggest health problems facing the world today. It is a condition in which excess body fat impacts a person's health. Obesity affects 33 percent of the world's population, or roughly 2.1 billion people.

Obesity is determined using a measure called body mass index (BMI), which is a calculation of a person's weight in kilograms divided by his or her height. The reason doctors use this calculation is that a person's weight alone is not enough information to determine whether the person is healthy or unhealthy. Muscle weighs more than fat, which means that a very athletic, muscular person might weigh more than you'd expect—but that doesn't mean the person is unhealthy. Someone with a BMI between 25 and 29.9 is considered overweight, and anything above 30 is in the category of obese.

Being overweight or obese is a serious health concern because of the many impacts that the extra weight has on the human body. Obesity can lead to a number of health issues, including diabetes, high blood pressure, heart disease, arthritis, stroke, and gout, a joint disorder. Moreover, the more weight people carry around with them, the more stress they put on their joints.

Researchers have also found a correlation between obesity and some types of cancer. In 2016 researchers reviewed more than 1,000 scientific studies and concluded that a person who is overweight or obese is at risk for at least 13 different types of cancer. Scientists had already known that if a person was overweight or obese he or she was at risk of five different cancers, including those of the esophagus, colon, breast, kidney, and uterus. The review, published in the *New England Journal of Medicine*, also showed a relationship between fat and eight additional cancers, including cancers of the gallbladder, pancreas, and thyroid, and a blood cancer called multiple myeloma.

CDC Growth Charts United States

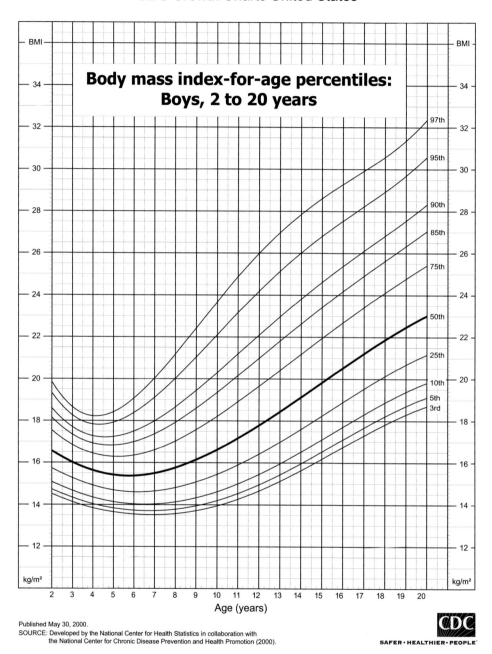

Body mass index-for-age percentiles: Boys, 2 to 20 years

Published May 30, 2000.
SOURCE: Developed by the National Center for Health Statistics in collaboration with
the National Center for Chronic Disease Prevention and Health Promotion (2000).

Because kids grow at different rates, there is no absolutely "correct" BMI for them. So BMIs for kids and teens are calculated and then placed on a scale for comparison to other kids.

CDC Growth Charts United States

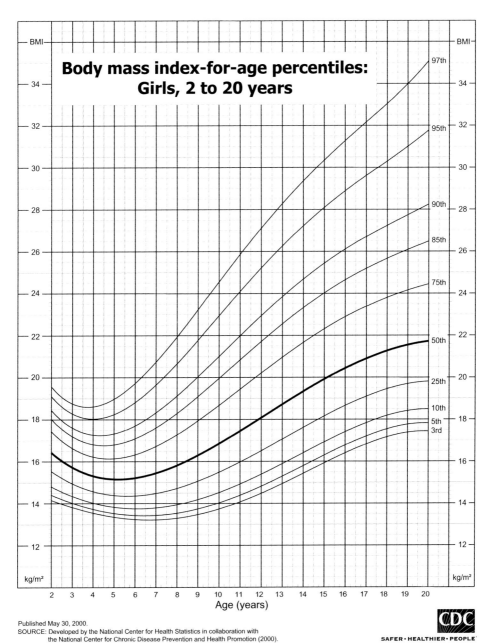

**Body mass index-for-age percentiles:
Girls, 2 to 20 years**

Boys and girls have different rates of growth, and therefore they have different BMI charts.

SUGAR, FAT, AND DIABETES

We cannot talk about obesity and fat without talking about sugar. Much like fat, sugar is not all bad. Sugar is a carbohydrate, and without carbohydrates the body would cease to function. While sugar in the right amounts is necessary for life, consuming too much of it can cause a variety of health problems.

Here's why: the body burns sugar as energy, known as glucose. Glucose fuels every process in the body, allowing cells to function and grow normally. However, the body turns extra sugar into fat, which it then stores for later use.

Flooding the body with processed sugar—the type of sugar you find in packaged food or in a sugar bowl—can overwhelm a person's metabolism. As a result, the body piles up the fat. Americans eat on average 22.7 teaspoons of sugar a day. Every teaspoon of processed sugar contains about 130 calories.

Sodas are very high in sugar, which can easily end up as fat on the body.

Most processed sugar is made up of equal amounts of glucose and fructose (fruit sugar). While the body's cells metabolize glucose, the liver is responsible for processing fructose. When the liver breaks fructose down, it produces triglycerides, the bad fat. While some of that fat can stay in the liver and damage it, most triglycerides enter the bloodstream.

Sugar is also a problem in low-fat meals. People who eat low-fat products might think they are doing something healthy, but that's not necessarily the case. Food manufacturers tend to pack their low-fat products with sugar to make them taste better. This means that the typical low-fat meal is high in carbs and calories. You can read more about the impact of low-fat diets on health in chapter four.

Researchers also say that obesity is the main cause of diabetes, a group of blood diseases caused by too much sugar in the bloodstream. Diabetes occurs when the system that regulates blood sugar fails because of a lack of *insulin*, a **hormone** produced in the pancreas that regulates the level of glucose in the blood. It also helps cells use glucose for energy.

When there is too little insulin, glucose cannot travel to the cells, disrupting the body's ability to burn glucose as energy. That's why diabetics must take insulin made in a laboratory. The Diabetes Research Institute Foundation says 380 million people around the world suffer from diabetes, including 29 million Americans.

Heart Disease

Moreover, a diet rich in saturated and trans fats can raise cholesterol levels in the blood, which can lead to heart disease. Heart disease can cause numerous problems, including **atherosclerosis**, a condition that develops when plaque builds up in the walls of arteries, making it difficult for blood to pass through. Plaque can stop the blood from flowing altogether, causing a heart attack.

By the same measure, unsaturated fats, especially those found in fish, nuts, seeds, and vegetables, can make a heart healthy. Essential fatty acids, which our bodies cannot make, improve cholesterol levels. However, doctors warn that if your total fat intake is more than 37 percent of all your total daily calories, and even if most of that fat comes in the form of unsaturated fats, you are still at an increased risk of having a heart attack. A person's saturated fat intake should not be more than 10 percent for people with diabetes or those in other high-risk groups.

High Blood Pressure

Extra weight can also cause high blood pressure, also known as hypertension. Blood pressure is the amount of force flowing blood puts on the walls of blood vessels.

Not all fat is bad for your heart—for example, salmon contains the heart-healthy fatty acid called omega-3.

When your heart beats, it pushes blood through a system of hollow blood tubes—arteries, capillaries, and veins. Arteries have thick walls. They carry blood from the heart to all parts of the body. Capillaries are like the thin branches of a tree that transport blood throughout tissue. Veins carry blood back to the heart.

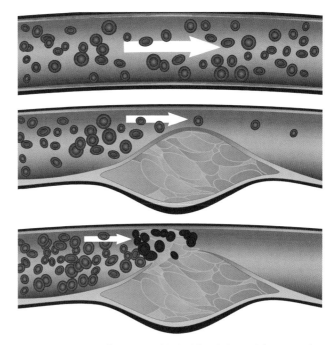

Artist rendering of an artery blocked by cholesterol (in orange).

Excess weight makes the heart work harder to pump the same amount of blood. Accordingly, blood pressure increases. High cholesterol can also cause blood pressure to increase. As plaque forms, artery walls narrow, which causes the heart to work harder to push blood throughout the body.

WHY ARE WE SO FAT?

There are various reasons why nearly a third of Americans are overweight and obese. The main reason is that we consume much more energy than we burn. To gain a pound of fat, a person has to eat 3,500 calories without burning those calories off by exercising. If we burn fewer calories than we consume, our bodies have to find a place to put all that excess energy. All that energy gets crammed into fat cells. Generally speaking, obese people have more fat cells than skinny people. Their fat cells are also larger.

Genetics also plays a role in obesity. Genes are inherited characteristics that are passed down from generation to generation. In recent years, scientists have found several dozen genes related to obesity.

Hormones also have an impact. In 1994 scientists discovered a hormone called *leptin* that affects how the body regulates weight. Leptin tells the brain to stop eating. When people have the right amount of leptin in their systems, they have an appropriate appetite. If leptin is not available or is available only in small amounts,

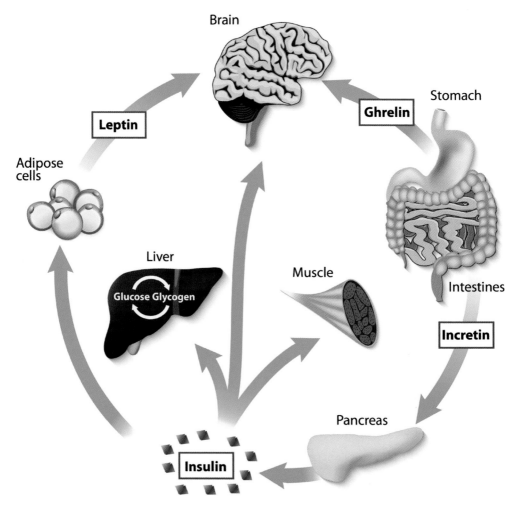

The human body uses hormones such as leptin to control appetite. Leptin is produced by fat cells.

OBESITY AMONG CHILDREN AND ADOLESCENTS

Obesity has become a major health issue for children and adolescents. According to the Centers for Disease Control and Prevention (CDC), during the past 30 years, the obesity rate for children and adolescents has quadrupled. In 1980 the obesity rate of children 6 to 11 years old was 7 percent. Today, it is around 18 percent. Similarly, the obesity rate of adolescents, aged 12–19, was 5 percent in 1980. Today, it is around 21 percent.

Doctors worry that many kids are not getting as much physical activity as they need.

a person's desire to eat will continue. However, obese people have a lot of leptin, yet they still gain weight. Why does that happen?

Leptin is produced by fat cells. The amount of leptin those cells release is directly related to the amount of body fat a person has. Obese people need more leptin than a person of average weight to signal the brain to stop eating.

EDUCATIONAL VIDEO

GOOD AND BAD FATS

Scan this code for a video about adding healthy fats to your diet.

Gender also plays a role. When girls are young, they tend to have 10 to 15 percent more body fat than boys. After puberty, the percentage jumps to 20 to 30 percent. When boys grow up, they generally produce more lean muscle. The extra fat in girls is a normal part of their development.

Eating processed foods also makes us fat. Processed foods are laden with hidden sugars. Whether Americans know it or not, we eat an average of 22.7 teaspoons of sugar a day. That's way too much, experts say. Every teaspoon of processed sugar (more on that later) contains about 130 calories and has zero nutritional value.

How Much Fat Should We Eat?

That's a good question. The American Heart Association and the National Institutes of Health say that a person should limit their daily intake of fat to 30 percent of their daily calories. However, this can be a double-edged sword. You can't stop eating fat entirely or your body won't function as it should.

A 2006 study published in the *Journal of the American Medical Association* found that 49,000 women who followed a low-fat diet were just as likely to have a heart attack, stroke, or other form of cardiovascular disease as women who did not follow such a diet.

"Over a mean of 8.1 years, a dietary intervention that reduced total fat intake and increased intakes of vegetables, fruits, and grains did not significantly reduce the risk of CHD (coronary heart disease), stroke, or CVD (cardiovascular disease) . . . suggesting that more focused diet and lifestyle interventions may be needed to improve risk factors and reduce CVD risk," the report concluded.

TEXT-DEPENDENT QUESTIONS

1. What is the difference between obesity and being overweight?
2. What are the jobs of each type of blood vessel: arteries, veins, capillaries?
3. What is leptin?

RESEARCH PROJECT

Complete this demonstration to find out how cholesterol can block your arteries.

What You Need

- scissors
- tape
- 2 plastic cups
- 1 straw with a small opening
- 1 straw with a wide opening
- water colored red with food coloring
- a pan

What to Do

Cut a hole close to the bottom of each of the plastic cups. Place the straw with the small opening through the hole in one cup. Place the straw with the large opening through the hole in the other cup. Place some tape around the opening and straw so the straw stays in place. Put the cups and the straws in the pan. Pour water into each of the cups. Watch what happens. How does this demonstration relate to what you've already read about the effects of cholesterol?

CHAPTER 4

CONSUMING FATS

 ## WORDS TO UNDERSTAND

reformulate: to make a change in the formula of a product.

salvo: here, a sudden act that starts a metaphorical battle.

If you ask any chef or baker, cooking with fat (trans or otherwise) is an art. Cooks simply cannot get along without it. They use large amounts of butter, shortening, margarine, and oils when they cook. Each of these fats has a different property that impacts the flavor, texture, and smell of food.

For example, bakers use shortening because it contains no water. Shortening is a saturated fat created from liquid oil by hydrogenation. It is solid at room temperature. Bakers will use shortening to make pie crusts, biscuits, and cream puffs. Shortening gives the crust a flaky texture because the fat reacts with proteins in flour. Shortening also adds flavor and is the main ingredient in frostings, fillings, and icings. It can also add air to cake batter. It makes it last longer when it comes out of the oven. It also helps other ingredients mix together.

Butter and margarine products contain moisture that produces a different texture than shortening. When the fat oil is added to batter, it traps tiny air bubbles that help batter to rise. Fat helps keep dough together and makes it easier for different flavors to blend. It also transfers heat during cooking, which is why you use a slab of butter to fry an egg or a tablespoon of vegetable oil to sauté garlic or mushrooms in a frying pan.

Chefs also take advantage of the fat that is already in certain ingredients. For example, fat helps determine the melting point of certain foods, such as chocolate.

Cooks use butter to add flavor, improve texture, and transfer heat.

Fat also increases calorie density in food. Foods with high calorie densities have more calories even though the weight of the food is less. This means people can consume more calories in smaller portions. While that might not seem like a good thing, calorie-dense food allows people in poor regions where caloric intake is low to consume more calories.

FATS AND PUBLIC HEALTH

It was 2006, and New York City was going where no city had gone before. In front of the city's Board of Health was a proposal to stop New York's 20,000 restaurants from using partially hydrogenated oils and spreads, the main sources of trans fats. The idea was to replace the unhealthy fat and spreads with healthier alternatives. The measure, experts said, would make people healthier.

Although some people, including many restaurant owners railed against the ban, many people seemed to agree it was a good idea. "Government intervention is one way of dealing with the health care crisis we are confronted with," one doctor wrote to the *New York Times*. "The city-wide requirement to replace trans-fat-bloated cooking oils with non-trans-fat cooking oils is the perfect balance of protection for the consumer and the restaurant owner," wrote another. "It takes a realistic approach to the use of these cooking oils. Since trans-fat-oils are unhealthy, it is necessary to ban them to improve the overall health of the citizens."

▼▼▼▼▼▼▼▼▼▼▼▼▼▼▼▼▼▼▼▼▼▼▼▼▼▼▼▼▼

USES OF FAT IN BAKING AND FRYING

 The following chart shows some of the basic uses and outcomes of fat in two types of cooking: baking and frying.

Fat	Baking	Frying
Butter	adds flavor and improvers texture of baked goods	can be used for sautéing, although it burns easily
Margarine spread (20%–60% fat)	creates cake-like texture, but is not recommended to be used for pie crusts	can be used for sautéing, but it is may not be the best option
Cooking oil	used for special recipes, along with box cake mixes, brownie mixes, and quick breads	sautéing, frying, and deep-fat frying
Shortening	produces flaky pie crust and thick frostings	sautéing, frying, and deep-fat frying
Cooking spray	keeps food from sticking	can be used to sauté in nonstick pans

Source: International Food Information Council Foundation, http://www.foodinsight.org/Content/6/FatsInFoods-Single.pdf.

▲▲▲▲▲▲▲▲▲▲▲▲▲▲▲▲▲▲▲▲▲▲▲▲▲▲▲▲▲

After New York passed its trans-fat ban, other cities and states, including Philadelphia and California, followed. Many fast-food restaurants, including McDonald's and Chick-fil-A, voluntarily removed trans fats from their menus. The ban, at least in New York, seemed to work. In 2012 the city reported that the average fat content of fast-food meals dropped from 3 grams to 0.5 grams.

Ridding menus of trans fats underscored just how seriously public health officials and restaurant owners were taking the impact of fat on people's lives. The laws were just one **salvo** in the ongoing battle of the bulge. In 2015 the Food and Drug Administration announced that food companies had to remove all trans fats from their foods within three years.

Each day in every community in every neighborhood in the world, people young and old, rich and poor, male and female, try to lose weight. In most cases, it is easier

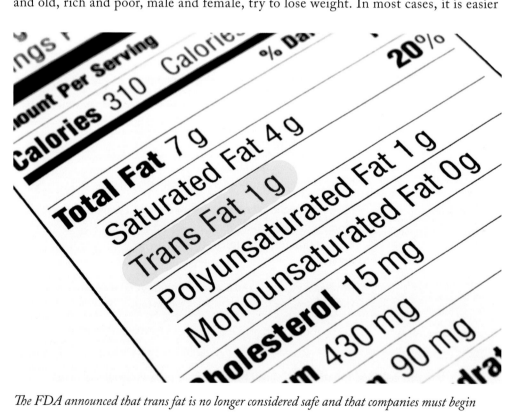

The FDA announced that trans fat is no longer considered safe and that companies must begin removing it from their products.

said than done. People go on low-fat or no-fat diets. They burn calories at the gym, on the ball field, and on the tennis court. They buy diet pills, exercise machines, and gym memberships. The Boston Medical Center estimates that 45 million Americans spend $33 billion per year on various weight-loss products.

Bad for the Economy

Reducing body fat is just not a matter of life and death, or good health versus ill health; it is also an economic issue. Obesity is a preventable disease, yet it is dragging many economies down. In the United States, for example, obesity is responsible for $147 to $210 billion a year in health-care costs, job absenteeism, and lower productivity at work. Obese workers spend 42 percent more on health care than those who are of a healthy weight.

In 2008 the New York Academy of Medicine and the Urban Institute found that a $10 investment per person in community-based programs designed to increase physical activity and improve nutrition could save $16 billion on health-care costs in the United States alone.

Healthy Eating in Schools

Even your schools have tried to get the fat out of your diet. It wasn't that long ago that students could buy pizza and hamburgers and other fat-laden food in school cafeterias. If you look at your school's lunch menu today, you'll see a lot more salads and sandwiches on whole-wheat bread. Schools have also begun to ban sugary soda.

Changing the menu options in schools didn't happen overnight. In 1966 President Lyndon Johnson signed into law the Child Nutrition Act to "help meet the nutritional needs of children." The act established the School Breakfast Program, which provided low-cost or free breakfasts to children.

The idea behind the law, according to the CDC, was to help children receive a healthful meal at the start of their day. A poor diet, experts maintained, led to a decline in energy throughout the day. As a result, hungry children did not do well in school.

In 2012 President Barack Obama signed the Healthy, Hunger-Free Kids Act. Greasy pizza, over-salted french fries, and fat-laden meals were replaced with more lean proteins, fruits, vegetables, and whole grains.

Many popular lunches were **reformulated** to become more healthful. For example, in one school district, a Philly cheesesteak sandwich was reengineered to include low-fat, low-salt processed cheese on a whole grain bun. Kids were given side dishes of green beans, canned peaches, and an apple.

While health and school experts applauded the law, most kids were not so enthusiastic. A story in the *New York Times* in 2015 highlighted that kids were throwing

Schools are working to reduce the amount of fat served at lunch.

their healthier meals away, presumably because those meals were not satisfying to them. When school officials looked closer at what children were eating at home, they found that most parents didn't serve healthful meals. Bertrand Weber, director of culinary and nutrition services at the Minneapolis Public Schools said this: "Other than mandating more fruits and vegetables, the new regulations haven't really changed anything except force manufacturers to re-engineer products" so they meet the federal guidelines, although the kids do not like them.

EDUCATIONAL VIDEO

SCHOOL LUNCHES

Scan this code for a video about school lunches.

The Problem with Low-Fat Diets

If reducing fat is a good way to stay healthy, then it's logical to assume that low-fat foods are good for you. Not necessarily. As you read earlier, healthy fat is good for you if consumed in the right amounts. Eliminating fat from your diet, however, will cause your body to function abnormally. If you don't eat enough of the right amount of fat, you're putting yourself at risk for not getting sufficient amounts of fat-soluble vitamins and important fatty acids.

You might also eat more processed low-fat food rather than healthier alternatives, such as fruits, vegetables, whole grains, and other food. Studies have shown that people eat 50 percent more processed food when they see labels such as "no-fat" or "low-fat." Consequently, they misjudge the calories they are eating, and consume far more than they should. Moreover, processed low-fat food contains refined sugar, a carbohydrate, which the body can process into additional fat.

Nutritionists recommend a healthy diet with lots of fruits and vegetables rather than "low-fat" prepackaged foods that may be high in sugar.

THE MEDITERRANEAN DIET

Some ways of eating have proved beneficial, especially the Mediterranean diet, which focuses on traditional foods and beverages consumed by those living in Crete, Greece, and southern Italy. What is so special about these countries? Compared to other regions, especially the United States, heart disease is uncommon for many people living in those areas. People there mostly eat a diet consisting of fruits, vegetables, fish, whole grains, breads, nuts and seeds, and large amounts of olive oil and canola oil, both unsaturated fats. They eat red meat sparingly.

Numerous studies have been conducted on the Mediterranean diet, and the results have been astounding. One of the most important was published in 2013 in the *New England Journal of Medicine*. In that study, researchers followed 7,447 people for five

Many of the foods that are part of the Mediterranean diet are high in omega-3 fatty acids.

years. One group ate a Mediterranean diet with added olive oil, while the others ate a Mediterranean diet with added nuts. A control group ate a low-fat diet.

When the results were tallied, researchers concluded that the risk of heart attack, stroke, and death from cardiovascular disease was reduced by 30 percent for those on the Mediterranean diet with added olive oil, and 28 percent for those on the Mediterranean diet with added nuts. Reducing fat-laden foods and replacing them with healthier alternatives such as fruits, nuts, whole grains, and vegetables might be hard to swallow at times, but at the end of the day, your heart and your waistline will thank you.

TEXT-DEPENDENT QUESTIONS

1. What reason did the U.S. government give when it started regulating school lunches?
2. Which city in the United States was the first to ban trans fats?
3. What is the Mediterranean diet, and why is it so intriguing to researchers?

RESEARCH PROJECT

Go to the World Obesity website (www.worldobesity.org/resources/world-map-obesity/) and compare the obesity rates for men and women in the United States, Great Britain, Egypt, Iraq, Australia, China, Canada, India, and Russia. Create a chart showing what you found. What can you conclude?

FURTHER READING

BOOKS AND ARTICLES

Enig, Mary G. *Know Your Fats: The Complete Primer for Understanding Nutrition of Fats, Oils and Cholesterol*. Silver Spring, MD: Bethesda Press, 2003.

Hamblin, James. "Science Compared Every Diet, and the Winner Is Real Food." *The Atlantic*, March 24, 2014. http://www.theatlantic.com/health/archive/2014/03/science-compared-every-diet-and-the-winner-is-real-food/284595/.

Harvard School of Public Health. "Fats and Cholesterol." https://www.hsph.harvard.edu/nutritionsource/what-should-you-eat/fats-and-cholesterol/.

Kostovski, Vlad. *All about Fats*. Amazon Digital, 2012.

Lawrence, Glen. *The Fats of Life: Essential Fatty Acids in Health and Disease*. New Brunswick, NJ: Rutgers University Press, 2010.

Mayo Clinic. "Mediterranean Diet: A Heart–Healthy Eating Plan." http://www.mayoclinic.org/healthy-lifestyle/nutrition-and-healthy-eating/in-depth/mediterranean-diet/art-20047801.

MedlinePlus. "Dietary Fats Explained." August 12, 2014. https://medlineplus.gov/ency/patientinstructions/000104.htm.

U.S. Department of Agriculture. "How Are Oils Different from Solid Fats?" https://www.choosemyplate.gov/oils-fats.

U.S. Food and Drug Administration. "FDA Cuts Trans Fat in Processed Food." http://www.fda.gov/ForConsumers/ConsumerUpdates/ucm372915.htm.

WEBSITES

American Heart Association

www.heart.org

Lots of information about heart health, including which fats to seek out and which to avoid.

Dairy Farmers of Canada–"Butter"

www.dairygoodness.ca/butter/types-of-butter

Everything you've always wanted to know about butter but were afraid to ask.

USDA: ChooseMyPlate.gov

www.choosemyplate.gov

Lots of information about the government's nutrition recommendations.

EDUCATIONAL VIDEOS

Chapter One: SciShow. "The Deal With Fat." https://www.youtube.com/watch?v=mvvx2yQRbzQ.

Chapter Two: AsapSCIENCE. "Butter vs Margarine." https://youtu.be/KG_ybdk1VaE.

Chapter Three: HealthNation. "Good Fats vs. Bad Fats." https://www.youtube.com/watch?v=3Gqo3Y6WFYA.

Chapter Four: *Bon Appétit*. "Kids Try 100 Years of Brown Bag Lunches from 1900 to 2000." https://youtu.be/vgZLPGT5llg.

SERIES GLOSSARY

amino acid: an organic molecule that is the building block of proteins.

antibody: a protein in the blood that fights off substances the body thinks are dangerous.

antioxidant: a substance that fights against free radicals, molecules in the body that can damage other cells.

biofortification: the process of improving the nutritional value of crops through breeding or genetic modification.

calories: units of energy.

caramelization: the process by which the natural sugars in foods brown when heated, creating a nutty flavor.

carbohydrates: starches, sugars, and fibers found in food; a main source of energy for the body.

carcinogen: something that causes cancer.

carnivorous: meat-eating.

cholesterol: a soft, waxy substance present in all parts of the body, including the skin, muscles, liver, and intestines.

collagen: a fibrous protein that makes up much of the body's connective tissues.

deficiency: a lack of something, such as a nutrient in one's diet.

derivative: a product that is made from another source; for example, malt comes from barley, making it a barley derivative.

diabetes: a disease in which the body's ability to produce the hormone insulin is impaired.

emulsifiers: chemicals that allow mixtures to blend.

enzyme: a protein that starts or accelerates an action or process within the body.

food additive: a product added to a food to improve flavor, appearance, nutritional value, or shelf life.

genetically modified organism (GMO): a plant or animal that has had its genetic material altered to create new characteristics.

growth hormone: a substance either naturally produced by the body or synthetically made that stimulates growth in animals or plants.

herbicide: a substance designed to kill unwanted plants, such as weeds.

ionizing radiation: a form of radiation that is used in agriculture; foods are exposed to X-rays or other sources of radiation to eliminate microorganisms and insects and make foods safer.

legume: a plant belonging to the pea family, with fruits or seeds that grow in pods.

macronutrients: nutrients required in large amounts for the health of living organisms, including proteins, fats, and carbohydrates.

malnutrition: a lack of nutrients in the diet, due to food inaccessibility, not consuming enough vitamins and minerals, and other factors.

marketing: the way companies advertise their products to consumers.

metabolism: the chemical process by which living cells produce energy.

micronutrients: nutrients required in very small amounts for the health of living organisms.

monoculture farming: the agricultural practice of growing a massive amount of a single crop, instead of smaller amounts of diverse crops.

nutritional profile: the nutritional makeup of given foods, including the balance of vitamins, minerals, proteins, fats, and other components.

obesity: a condition in which excess body fat has amassed to the point where it causes ill-health effects.

pasteurization: a process that kills microorganisms, making certain foods and drinks safer to consume.

pesticide: a substance designed to kill insects or other organisms that can cause damage to plants or animals.

processed food: food that has been refined before resale, often with additional fats, sugars, sodium, and other additives.

protein complementation: the dietary practice of combining different plant-based foods to get all of the essential amino acids.

refined: when referring to grains or flours, describing those that have been processed to remove elements of the whole grain.

savory: a spicy or salty quality in food.

subsidy: money given by the government to help industries and businesses stay competitive.

sustainable: a practice that can be successfully maintained over a long period of time.

vegan: a person who does not eat meat, poultry, fish, dairy, or other products sourced from animals.

vegetarian: a person who does not eat meat, poultry, or fish.

whole grain: grains that have been minimally processed and contain all three main parts of the grain—the bran, the germ, and the endosperm.

INDEX

A

adipose cells, 31–32

advertising. *See* labels

American Heart
Association, 42

Americans
fat consumption, 9–10, 12,
19
sugar consumption, 36,
42

Arkansas, 28

arteries, 9, 39
clogged, 10, 31
hardening of
(atherosclerosis), 31, 37
high blood pressure, 39
LDL, 14, 15
plaque, 14, 15, 37, 39

artificial trans fat. *See*
hydrogenation

atherosclerosis (hardening of
arteries), 31, 37

B

"bad cholesterol." *See* LDL
(low-density lipoprotein)

baked goods, 10, 12, 17, 47

BMI. *See* body mass index
(BMI)

body mass index (BMI), 33,
34–35

bread, 47

brownie mix, 47

burning off calories, activity
level, 39, 41

butter
cooking/baking, 45, 46, 4
7
Crisco as alternative,
27–28
substitute, 24–25
vs. margarine, 25–27

C

cake, 10, 17, 45

cake mix, 47

calorie density, 46

calories, 9
fat, storage of extra
calories, 9, 12, 16, 31

cancer and obesity, 33

canola oil, 17, 20, 53

capillaries, 39

carbohydrates, 9
macronutrient, 11

carbon, hydrogen, and
oxygen atoms
fatty acids, 15
glycerides, 14
saturated fats, 16, 33

cardiovascular disease
(CVD), 42, 54

caul fat, 23, 26

Centers for Disease Control
and Prevention (CDC)
children, obesity rate, 41

growth charts, body mass
index, 34–35

CHD. *See* coronary heart
disease (CHD)

cheese, 10, 17
Philly cheesesteak
sandwich, 50

chicken, dark meat, 10

Chick-fil-A, 48

Child Nutrition Act, 49

children and adolescents
body mass index (BMI),
33, 34–35
burning off calories,
activity level, 39, 41
obesity rate, 41
public schools, 49–51
school lunches, 50–51

cholesterol, 14–15
HDL, 14, 15
LDL, 14–15
plaque, 14, 15, 37, 39
triglycerides, 14, 17, 31, 37

compound lipids, 14

cookies, 10, 12, 17, 28

cooking/baking, 45–47

cooking oils & sprays, 47

coronary heart disease
(CHD), 18, 42

Crisco, 27–28

crystallized cottonseed oil
(Crisco), 27–28

cupcakes, 10, 17

CVD. *See* cardiovascular
disease (CVD)

D
diabetes, 9, 10
  insulin, 9, 37
  obesity, 33, 37
  saturated fat, 38
  sugar, 36–37
  trans fat, 18
donuts, 17

E
economic impact of being
  overweight & obesity, 49
energy
  metabolism, 9, 16, 31
  source of, fatty acids, 16
Europe, obesity statistics,
  20–21

F
fast food
  banning trans fat, 48
  French fries, 18, 28, 29, 50
  partially hydrogenated oil,
  29
  reusing trans oils, 18
fast food restaurants
  Chick-fil-A restaurants, 48
  McDonald's, 29, 48
  reusing trans fat oils, 18
  trans fat removed from
  menus, 48
fat
  atomic makeup, 14, 15, 16,
  33
  basics (video), 12

fatty acids, 15–17
glycerides, 14
Good and Bad Fats (video),
  42
hidden fat, 12
lipids, 14
macronutrient, 11
role of, 11, 12–13
taste, 12
trans fat, 17–21
fat consumption
  average Americans, 9–10,
  12
  calorie density, increase in,
  46
  cooking & baking, 45–46,
  47
  excess consumption, 9–10
  how much should we eat,
  42
  low-fat diets, 51–52
  Mediterranean diet, 53–54
  public health, 46–48
  public schools, 49–51
  saturated fat, 19
fat storage
  as energy, 9, 12, 16, 31
  body mass index (BMI),
  33, 34–35
  cancer and obesity, 33
  dangers of too much fat,
  31, 33–35
  heart disease, 37–38
  men, 32
  metabolism, 9, 16, 31
  obesity *vs.* overweight, 33
  women, 32
fatty acids, 15–17

atomic makeup, 15
monosaturated fat, 16, 17
omega-3, 17, 38, 53
saturated fat, 16–17
unsaturated fat, 16, 17
FDA. *See* Food and Drug
  Administration (FDA)
first manufactured food to
  contain trans fat, 28
Food and Drug
  Administration (FDA)
  trans fat, 19, 20, 48
food manufacturers, 17–19,
  27–28
France, 1800s, 24–25
French fries, 18, 28, 29, 50
frosting, 45, 47
fructose, 37
frying, 47
  Crisco, 27–28
  French fries, 18, 28, 29, 50

G
gender and obesity, 42
genetics and obesity, 40–42
glucose, 36, 37
glycerides, 14
  atomic makeup, 14
  triglycerides, 14, 17, 31,
  37
Good and Bad Fats (video),
  42
"good cholesterol." *See*
  HDL (high-density
  lipoprotein)
"good fat." *See* unsaturated fat
  ("good fat")
gout, 33

INDEX

H

hardening of arteries (atherosclerosis), 31, 37

HDL (high-density lipoprotein), 14, 15

saturated fat, 16–17

health care costs and obesity, 49

health issues. *See also* heart disease

body mass index (BMI), 33, 34–35

cancer and obesity, 33

dangers of too much fat, 31, 33–35

high blood pressure, 38–39

obesity *vs.* overweight, 33

partially hydrogenated oil, 19, 20

trans fat, study on impact of, 18–19

Healthy, Hunger-Free Kids Act, 50–51

heart disease. *See also* arteries

atherosclerosis, 31, 37

cardiovascular disease (CVD), 42, 54

coronary heart disease (CHD), 18, 42

dangers of too much fat, 37–38

impact of trans fat, study, 18–19

increased risk, 18–19

plaque, 14, 15, 37, 39

saturated fat, 37

trans fat, 18–19, 37

unsaturated fat, 37–38

hidden fat, 12

hidden sugar, 42

high blood pressure (hypertension) and obesity, 38–39

high cholesterol, 39

high-fat diet, 14

hormones, 31

cholesterol, 14

insulin, 9, 37

leptin, 40–42

Hubbard, Governor Lucius, 25

humans

early ancestors, protein craving, 23–24

modern humans, 24

hydrogenation, 17–19, 27–29

Crisco, 27–28

food manufacturers, 27–28

partially hydrogenated oil, 19, 20, 29, 46–48

process of, 17–19

reusing trans fat/oils, 18

texture of, 17

hypertension (high blood pressure), causes, 38–39

I

ice cream, 11

Illinois, 28

Industrial Age, 23, 24

Johnson, President Lyndon, 49

Journal of the American Medical Association, 42

K

kids & teens

burning off calories, activity level, 39, 41

growth charts, body mass index, 33, 34–35

obesity rate, 41

public schools, 49–51

school lunches, 50–51

L

labels

trans fat, 20

LDL (low-density lipoprotein), 14–15

arteries, 14, 15

plaque, 14, 15, 37, 39

trans fat, 18

leptin hormone, 40–42

lipids

compound lipids, 14

simple lipids, 14

low-fat diet, 42, 49

fats, 51–52

Mediterranean diet *vs.*, 54

low-fat products, 36–37

M

macronutrients, 9, 11

margarine

"butter wars," 25–27

creation of, 24–25

France, 1800s, 24–25

oleomargarine, 25

partially hydrogenated oil, 29

World War II, 29

Margarine Act, 27

Massachusetts, 28

McDonald's
  partially hydrogenated oil,
    29
  trans fat removed from
    menus, 48

meat
  early ancestors, 23–24
  red meat, 17, 53

Mediterranean diet, 53–54

Megè-Mouriès, Hippolyte,
  25

men, fat storage, 32

metabolism, 9, 16, 31
  storing and using fat, 9, 16,
    31
  too much sugar, 36–37

milk, 10, 17

Minnesota, 25

modern humans, 24

monosaturated fat, 16, 17

Mozaffarian, Dariush, 18–19

N

Napoleon III of France,
  24–25

National Institutes of
  Health, 42

naturally occurring trans
  fat, 17

*New England Journal of
  Medicine,* 53

New Jersey, 28

New York
  butter *vs.* margarine,
    26–27
  fattiest foods, 28

New York City

partially hydrogenated oil,
  banned, 46–48

New York Times, 47, 50–51

Normann, Wilhelm, 27

O

Obama, President Barack,
  50

obesity, 9
  body mass index (BMI),
    33, 34–35
  burning off calories,
    activity level, 39, 41
  children, obesity rate for,
    41
  diabetes, 33, 37
  economic impact, 49
  gender, 42
  genetics, 40–42
  health care costs, 49
  high blood pressure,
    38–39
  leptin hormone, 40–42
  mortality rate, Western
    Europe, 21
  obesity *vs.* overweight, 33
  processed foods, 42
  reasons why, 39–42
  sugar and, 36–37
  WHO, obesity statistics in
    Europe, 20–21

oleomargarine, 25

olive oil, 16, 17, 53, 54

omega-3 fatty acid, 17, 38, 53

overweight, 39–42. *See also*
  obesity
  body mass index (BMI),
    33, 34–35

burning off calories,
  activity level, 39, 41

economic impact, 49

gender, 42

genetics, 40–42

health care costs, 49

high blood pressure,
  38–39

leptin hormone, 40–42

main reason, 39

mortality rate, Western
  Europe, 21

obesity *vs.* overweight, 33

processed foods, 42

reasons why, 39–42

sugar, 36–37

P

partially hydrogenated oil
  ban of, 46–48
  FDA, food companies to
    remove, 48
  health issues, 19, 20
  margarine made from, 29
  popularity of, 29

peanuts, 10, 28

Philly cheesesteak sandwich,
  50

pie crust, 45, 47

plaque, 14, 15, 37, 39

polyunsaturated fat, 17
  canola oil, 17, 20, 53
  omega-3, 17, 38, 53

primates, 23, 24

processed foods, 42

processed sugars, 36–37

Proctor & Gamble, 27

proteins, 9

early ancestors, protein craving, 23–24

macronutrient, 11

public health, 46–48

public schools

fat consumption, 49–51

school lunches, 50–51

pudding, 12, 17

Q

Quarles, Senator Joseph, 26

R

red meat, 17, 23–24, 53

restaurants

Chick-fil-A restaurants, 48

McDonald's, 29, 48

partially hydrogenated oil, ban of, 46–48

reusing trans fat oils, 18

trans fat removed from menus, 48

S

salmon, 38

saturated fat, 16–17

atomic makeup, 16, 33

consumption of average Americans, 19

dangers of too much fat, 31, 33–35

diabetes, 38

HDL, 16–17

School Breakfast Program, 49–50

school lunches, 50–51

shortening

cooking/baking, 45, 47

Crisco, 27–28

simple lipids, 14

soda, 36, 49

steak, marbling, 13

stroke, 15, 31, 33, 42, 54

plaque, 14, 15, 37, 39

sugar, 36–37

consumption of average Americans, 36, 42

hidden sugar, 42

obesity and, 36–37

processed sugars, 36–37

soda, 36, 49

T

trans fat

artificial trans fat, creation of, 17–19

banning, 19–21

Crisco, 28

dangers of, generally, 17–19

dangers of too much, 31, 33–35

diabetes, 18

fast food restaurants reusing, 18

FDA, 19, 20, 48

first manufactured food to contain, 28

heart disease, 37

hydrogenation, 17–19, 27–29

impact on health, study, 18–19

labels, 20

LDL levels, 18

naturally occurring, 17

partially hydrogenated oil, 19, 20, 29, 46–48

WHO, Europe, 20–21

triglycerides, 14, 17, 31, 37

U

unsaturated fat ("good fat"), 16, 17

heart disease, 37–38

monosaturated fat, 16, 17

U.S. fattiest foods, 28

U.S. Supreme Court, "pink laws" overturned, 27

W

Weber, Bertrand, 51

weight. See obesity; overweight

Western Europe, obesity statistics, 21

WHO. See World Health Organization (WHO)

Wisconsin, 26, 27

women, fat storage, 32

World Health Organization (WHO)

Europe, obesity statistics, 20–21

World War II, butter shortage, 29

ABOUT THE AUTHOR

John Perritano is an award-winning journalist, writer, and editor from Southbury, CT. He has written numerous articles and books on a variety of subjects including science, sports, history, and culture for such publishers as Mason Crest, National Geographic, Scholastic, and Time/Life. His articles have appeared on Discovery.com, Popular Mechanics.com, and other magazines and websites. He holds a Master's Degree in American History from Western Connecticut State University.

PHOTO CREDITS